52 WEEKS
WITH JESUS
for KiDS

A DEVOTIONAL

JAMES MERRITT

HARVEST HOUSE PUBLISHERS
EUGENE, OREGON

Cover by Design by Julia, Woodland Park, Colorado

Published in association with the literary agency of Wolgemuth & Associates, Inc.

52 WEEKS WITH JESUS FOR KIDS

Copyright © 2016 James Merritt
Published by Harvest House Publishers
Eugene, Oregon 97402
www.harvesthousepublishers.com

ISBN 978-0-7369-6697-9 (pbk.)
ISBN 978-0-7369-6698-6 (eBook)

Library of Congress Cataloging-in-Publication Data
Names: Merritt, James Gregory, 1952- author.
Title: 52 weeks with Jesus for kids / James Merritt.
Other titles: Fifty two weeks with Jesus for kids
Description: Eugene, Oregon : Harvest House Publishers, 2016.
Identifiers: LCCN 2016013349 (print) | LCCN 2016031238 (ebook) | ISBN
    9780736966979 (pbk.) | ISBN 9780736966986 ()
Subjects: LCSH: Christian children—Prayers and devotions—Juvenile
    literature.
Classification: LCC BV4870 .M44 2016 (print) | LCC BV4870 (ebook) | DDC
    242/.62—dc23
LC record available at https://lccn.loc.gov/2016013349

Printed in the United States of America

16 17 18 19 20 21 22 23 24 / BP-CD / 10 9 8 7 6 5 4 3 2 1

This book is dedicated to Pop's four best buddies—
Harper, Casady, Presley, and Connor.
May you always walk with Jesus.

Contents

How to Read This Book

Are you ready to learn about Jesus and grow in your faith? In this book, you'll find 52 devotions all about Jesus and you. You can read one devotion a week—maybe on Sunday evenings, or whenever you like—and learn a ton about Jesus in a year. (Remember, a year has 52 weeks.) Or you can read the book at a quicker pace. It's totally up to you!

You might also want to get together with some friends to read the book. It would be fun to go through it with your Sunday school class, small group, or Bible club if you're involved in one of those. Another great option is to grab a pen and notebook so you can journal as you read. Once again, it's totally up to you!

No matter what you choose, enjoy your time discovering Jesus and learning how He wants to help you live your best life every single day.

1

We Are Family!

*But to all who believed him and accepted him,
he gave the right to become children of God.*

—John 1:12

If you're like a lot of people, your favorite holiday is Christmas. There's so much to love about that season, especially celebrating the birth of Jesus with family and friends.

On December 25, we remember that day thousands of years ago when Jesus was born. And while every child's birth is a very special event, the birth of Jesus was not your typical birth. People had been looking forward to it for more than four thousand years. That's a long time to be expecting a baby!

Have you ever made a family tree? A family tree lists your parents, your grandparents, your great-grandparents, and all your relatives as far back as you can find them. The very beginning of the New Testament lists the names of everyone in Jesus's family tree. Way back at the beginning of time, God made a promise that He would one day send a king who would be the Savior of the world.

God doesn't do anything randomly. He always had a plan and a purpose for Jesus, and He always has a plan and a purpose for us.

If you've accepted Jesus into your heart, you're also a part of God's family. Jesus's family tree is your family tree! No matter who your family is and no matter how much of your family tree you can draw, God is happy to welcome you into His family. You're an important branch on His tree, and He has an amazing plan for your life.

Being a part of the family of God is so awesome that we don't have to wait until December 25 to celebrate. We can celebrate being a part of His family every day of the year!

▶ **Jesus, thank You that I am part of Your family and that I can celebrate You every day of the year!**

Take This with You

God's family tree is the best place to be.

God Loves Misfits

But God is so rich in mercy, and he loved us so much, that
even though we were dead because of our sins, he gave
us life when he raised Christ from the dead.

—Ephesians 2:4-5

You might think someone as amazing as Jesus would
have come from a line of rich and famous people who
totally followed God and never did anything wrong, but
that's actually not true at all. Some of the people in Jesus's
family tree were poor. Others were thought of as different
or strange. Some were big-time sinners. You can even add
wicked kings to the bunch. The truth is, Jesus came from a
long line of misfits!

Your family doesn't have a lot of money? No problem!
Jesus Himself was born in a stable, the son of a carpenter,
not a prince who was born in a palace. You're not the most
popular person in your class? That's just fine! Jesus wasn't
very popular with His own people. Your best friend isn't
speaking to you? Not to worry! Jesus knew what it was like
to have a best friend turn on Him.

Want to know something really crazy? Jesus was a misfit.
Totally telling the truth here! No, He didn't sin. But He did

His own thing. He didn't act the way people expected Him to act. He didn't hang out with the people others expected Him to hang out with. He may not have even looked the way people expected Him to look. The people were expecting a powerful king, not some carpenter-turned-teacher who was leading around a sketchy group of followers. You might even call Him the "misfit Messiah."

That's good news for us! You can be exactly who you are, and God will love you. You don't have to look perfect. You don't have to act perfect. You don't have to be perfect at all. You just have to believe that Jesus—who *was* perfect—was the Son of God and that He died for your sins (your imperfections). That's all that matters to Him!

▶ **Jesus, thank You for Your love and grace. Thank You that I don't have to be perfect and that You love me and accept me just the way I am.**

Take This with You

Even though I'm not perfect,
God still loves me.

You Are Royalty!

The LORD will hold you in his hand for all to see—
a splendid crown in the hand of God.

—Isaiah 62:3

Have you ever dreamed of living in a castle and having an entire kingdom to call your own? It would be fun to be royalty, wouldn't it?

Actually, you probably *are* royalty! People who study the history of families have figured out that every person on earth is no doubt descended from one royal person or another. You are royalty and don't even know it! I bet you had no idea you have the blood of some king or queen flowing through your veins.

What's even better, if you believe in Jesus and are a part of His family, you're part of the greatest royal family ever. You're descended not just from any old king but from *the* King of kings.

It's pretty amazing to realize you're part of the royal family of God, isn't it? And, even better, you can personally know the King himself. Jesus tells us, "I love you. I want to be your Savior. I want to save you from your sins. You are important to My heart."

Can you imagine a king coming down from his lavish castle to live among the common people? Giving up his banquet table with all that fancy food and living on bread and water with those who couldn't afford much? Can you imagine a king leaving his luxurious robes and treasury of jewels behind and dressing in ordinary—or even tattered—clothing and wandering from place to place, not really having a home? That's what Jesus did. He did it for you and me.

It might be a little bit hard to understand why Jesus chose to become human and live in our world. The important thing is that you understand *why* He did it—because He loves us and wants us all to be a part of His royal family.

▶ **Jesus, thank You for becoming part of the human family so I could become a part of Your royal heavenly family. Teach me how to live for You, love You, and do Your will.**

Take This with You

If I am a child of God, I am a son or daughter of royalty. I am a prince or a princess!

4

Bread for the Journey

Jesus replied, "I am the bread of life.
Whoever comes to me will never be hungry again.
Whoever believes in me will never be thirsty."

—John 6:35

Can you remember the last time you ate some bread? Maybe you ate a bagel with cream cheese for breakfast. Or a sandwich for lunch. And there's that yummy, buttery garlic bread you enjoy with a spaghetti dinner. Just go to a grocery store or restaurant to see how much bread people eat every day—pancakes and waffles and French toast, sandwiches and wraps, pizza and biscuits. Bread is everywhere! Even if people don't have very much to eat, they almost always have bread.

When Jesus said, "I am the bread of life," I'm guessing He got some confused looks. How could a person be bread? We don't know for sure what Jesus looked like, but I'm certain He didn't look like a tortilla or a dinner roll!

But think about it this way. Bread is the one thing most humans share in common. If poor people don't have anything else, they probably have bread. Rich people who have everything else will usually also eat bread. Even if you can't eat gluten, you can probably eat gluten-free bread. Bread is important to life. And, like bread, Jesus is essential for life!

Hunger—for things like bread—is something God built into our bodies to remind us to eat. After all, we'll die without food. God has also built another kind of hunger into our bodies—the hunger for Jesus Christ, the Bread of Life. That kind of hunger is only satisfied by having a relationship with Jesus—praying, reading our Bible, and putting our trust in Him.

The next time you eat a piece of bread, thank God for giving you both food for your body and Jesus—the Bread of Life—for your soul.

▶ **Thank You, Jesus, for giving me not only bread to eat but also for giving me the gift of You—the Bread of Life. With You, I will never go hungry.**

Take This with You

Jesus satisfies the hunger of my heart.

Turn on the Light

Jesus spoke to the people once more and said,
"I am the light of the world. If you follow me,
you won't have to walk in darkness, because you will
have the light that leads to life."

—John 8:12

Years ago, I visited a place called Mammoth Cave. It was the first and only time I was ever in a cavern like that, and I'll never forget it. We descended deep into the cave, and then—without any warning—the guide turned off his flashlight. Talk about freaky!

Being in complete darkness is super scary. You feel helpless. You have no idea what's around you. But physical darkness—like the darkness in the cave—is nothing compared to spiritual darkness. When you're in spiritual darkness, you don't have any hope or joy. It's a scary place to be.

What do you do at home when the power goes out and you need to see? Do you try to sweep out the darkness with a broom or vacuum it away? No, you wouldn't do anything silly like that. You would turn on a flashlight or light a candle. The only thing that gets rid of darkness is light!

In John 8:12, Jesus doesn't just say He is a light. He says

He is *the* light. And He doesn't just say He is the light for some people in some places—like in a creepy cave. He's the light of the entire world.

Because Jesus is always with us, we always have a source of light. And when we believe in Him and follow Him, we shine His light in the dark too. The more lights that shine, the brighter the world becomes.

Escaping from darkness is as easy as turning on the light!

▶ **Jesus, shine Your light in my heart and life. And help me shine Your light for others.**

Take This with You

Jesus wants me to shine His light for others.

A Safe Place

I tell you the truth, I am the gate for the sheep. All who
came before me were thieves and robbers. But the
true sheep did not listen to them. Yes, I am the gate.
Those who come in through me will be saved. They
will come and go freely and will find good pastures.

—John 10:7-9

Do you have any animals? If you do, you know they need care. The goldfish needs to be fed. A dog needs food and water daily, and it also needs to be walked. Chickens need to be fed and watered, their eggs must be collected, and they need to be shut in every night.

And what about sheep? How do you take care of them? If you're a shepherd—someone who takes care of sheep— you need to give them food and water, of course. But probably your most important job is getting them safely into their pen at night. Back in Bible times, the sheep pen wasn't a big red barn. It was a space out in a field where, on four sides, rocks would be piled about a foot high, with a small opening on one side where the sheep would go in at night. The shepherd would lie down at that opening and become *the gate* for the flock. Nothing could go in or out unless the shepherd let it.

That's what Jesus meant when He said, "I am the gate for the sheep." Jesus is the shepherd and we are His sheep. He keeps us—His sheep—safe all the time.

If sheep know the shepherd is protecting them, they feel safe to come and go and wander in and out of the pen. If we know Jesus is protecting us, we'll feel safe as we come and go different places—from home to school, from school to a friend's house, from church to summer camp. As long as you know Jesus is your "gate"—your safe place—you will feel cared for and loved.

▶ **Jesus, thank You that You are my gate to a wonderful life and that You have invited me to enter in. I trust You to care for me.**

Take This with You

If Jesus is the gate for my life,
I'll always be protected.

7

Life Is Good

*I am the good shepherd; I know my own sheep, and
they know me, just as my Father knows me and I know
the Father. So I sacrifice my life for the sheep.*

—John 10:14-15

Have you ever had a really great teacher or coach who knew just what to do for every student or player? It's fun being in a class or on a team when someone who truly cares about everyone and knows what they're doing is in charge. They make class or practice fun. You're learning and improving, and life is good!

Jesus is like that really great teacher or coach—only better. In the Bible, He's called the "good shepherd." Two things make a shepherd *good*. He always leads the sheep where they need to go, and he always gives the sheep what they need to have. And that's why life is so good when you follow Jesus. You'll always go where you need to go, and you'll always have what you need to have.

The Good Shepherd—Jesus—also promises to be with you when you're worried or anxious or sad. He will give you *faith* that gets rid of fear. When you understand that you're kind of like a sheep and you need someone to guide you and take care of you, it's comforting to know Jesus is always there to be your shepherd. And sheep never need to be afraid when the Good Shepherd is near.

It's important to remember that shepherds can't *always* keep the bad things away from sheep. You'll still run into mean kids. You'll still sometimes forget to do your homework. You'll still sometimes not get along with your brother or your sister. But Jesus will always be there to help turn you around and get you headed back in the right direction.

Like that great teacher, Jesus knows exactly what you need. He invites you to make Him the Good Shepherd in your life and become part of His flock. Life is good when the Good Shepherd is in charge!

▶ Jesus, I am like a lost sheep without You. Today and every day, I need You to guide me and feed me. Thank You for being the Good Shepherd.

Take This with You

Life is good when I decide to follow the Shepherd who is good.

The Waiting Game

Wait patiently for the LORD. Be brave and
courageous. Yes, wait patiently for the LORD.

—Psalm 27:14

Have you ever spent a long time waiting for something,
like Christmas or your birthday or a really fun trip?
Waiting is hard!

Did you know Jesus sometimes made people wait?
Maybe someone was sick. Or worried. Or they needed something. While He *could* have come right away, sometimes He
chose not to. He wasn't doing it to be mean. He was just following God's lead and waiting for the perfect timing. It was
hard for His friends back then to understand why He made
them wait, just like it's hard for us to understand today.

We don't like to wait. But when we do have to wait, something happens. Waiting makes us more patient. Waiting
helps us trust Jesus. Waiting helps us really think about—
and appreciate—what we're waiting for. If summer vacation or your birthday just happened whenever you wanted
it to, it wouldn't be as special, would it?

When you're waiting for a hard situation to change, it's
important to remember that God's main concern is not

always making things all "better" right away. While He does have the ability to do that, it's not always His plan. Sometimes He has a better plan for us. Sometimes He wants us to learn and grow. Sometimes we never quite figure it out, but we still need to trust that He has a reason.

So what are some things you can do while you're waiting? You can talk to God about how you're feeling. You can read your Bible. You can focus on other people—like your friends and your family. And remember this: *No matter how long you wait, God is never late.*

▶ **Jesus, please help me to be patient as I wait for You. Fill my heart with the reminder that You are always on time.**

Take This with You

No matter what I'm facing or how long I've been waiting, God is never late.

One Way

Jesus told him, "I am the way, the truth, and the life.
No one can come to the Father except through me."

—John 14:6

Have you ever heard of the famous Lombard Street in San Francisco? Even though it's only one block long, people come from all over the world to see it, take pictures of it, and drive down it. And you can only drive *down* it because it's way too steep for cars to drive on it in both directions. Because it's so fun to drive, nobody complains that you can't go *up* Lombard Street.

Jesus is kind of like Lombard Street. People from all over the world come to Him, and He's the only street that leads to God. Jesus claimed, "No one can come to the Father except through me" (John 14:6).

You can get to Lombard Street by driving there. You get to God's one-way street by going to Jesus, who died on the cross to pay for everything you've ever done—and will do—wrong.

If you've ever been out hiking or exploring, you might know what it's like to get lost. At first you know where you're going, then you *think* you know where you're going, and finally you realize you have no clue where you're going— or where you are. Then what? The best way to stop being lost is to get found. Maybe a nice hiker leads you out of the woods. Once someone shows you the way, you aren't lost anymore.

Jesus does even more than this when you're lost. He doesn't just say, "I'll show you the way." He says, "I *am* the way."

When you travel with Jesus on His one-way street, you'll never be lost and you'll always be headed in the right direction.

▶ **Jesus, I believe You are the way. Help me to follow You, and give me the courage to tell my friends about You and lead them to You.**

Take This with You

Jesus doesn't just show you the way.
He *is* the way!

Fruit

I am the true grapevine, and my Father is the
gardener. He cuts off every branch of mine that
doesn't produce fruit, and he prunes the branches
that do bear fruit so they will produce even more.

—John 15:1-2

Fresh fruit—yum! Cherries and berries in the spring and early summer. Melons and grapes in the late summer. Apples and pears in the autumn. I'm getting hungry just thinking about all that delicious fruit!

Did you know growing fruit takes a lot of work? The gardener has to prune the tree or trim the vine and work the soil so lots of tasty fruit will grow. In the Bible, Jesus teaches that God is the gardener, Jesus is the vine, and we are the branches. The gardener's main job is to get the branches to grow lots of delicious fruit. And by *fruit*, the Bible means the qualities of Christ—things like kindness and patience and faithfulness.

One sure sign you're following Jesus is that your life is bearing fruit others can see. You're showing kindness to your siblings. You're obedient to your parents. You're a good friend. When you are connected to the root of Christ, you will bear the fruit of Christ.

When Jesus teaches that God is a gardener, He reminds us that God cares for us and wants us to be fruitful—to grow a lot of the right kind of fruit. What do you get from an apple tree? Apples, of course. And a pear tree always produces pears. A tomato plant won't ever produce watermelon, and you don't find strawberries growing on a cherry tree. In the same way, if we are the branches of the Jesus vine, our fruit should look like Jesus.

Just like a well-tended cherry tree will give you tons of sweet cherries in the summer, a life tended by Jesus will result in a bumper crop of good *spiritual* fruit—things like love, gentleness, peace, patience, faithfulness, self-control, goodness, and kindness.

If you're attached to the vine of Christ, you will bear the fruit of Christ!

▶ **Jesus, thank You for growing all sorts of good fruit in my life. Help me stay connected to You so I will continue to grow and thrive.**

Take This with You

When you connect to the vine of Christ, you bear the fruit of Christ.

It's a Miracle!

You are the God who performs miracles;
you display your power among the peoples.

—Psalm 77:14 NIV

That was a miracle!" Have you ever heard anyone say that? I have! Most of the time what the person is talking about isn't *really* a miracle. It's usually something like making a last-second shot in a basketball game or doing a good job on a test they thought they were going to fail. That's what most people mean when they talk about something being a miracle.

Miracles in the Bible are a much bigger deal. In fact, the Bible *begins* with a miracle: God creating the world. How crazy is that? Can you imagine saying some words and having this entire world pop up—plants, animals, people, and all? God was able to create something out of nothing. Talk about a miracle!

And then there are all the miracles Jesus did—giving sight to the blind, feeding the five thousand, even raising people from the dead. Not exactly your everyday stuff! And what's even more amazing is that He didn't do those things to call attention to Himself and show His followers how cool

He was. He did those things to point the way to God and to prove that what He said was true.

The ultimate purpose of everything Jesus said and did was to glorify His Father. Matthew 9:8 tells what happened when people witnessed one of Jesus's miracles: "They praised God for sending a man with such great authority."

Some people think miracles don't happen anymore now that we have the Bible. After all, the Bible gives us proof that Jesus is the Son of God, which is what Jesus was showing when He performed miracles. But God does still perform miracles today so we can see how wonderful and good and loving He is. And that's why we can—and should—still expect miracles. They really and truly happen!

▶ **Jesus, because of the miracles You've done in the past, I believe You are who You say You are. You are the giver of all good things!**

Take This with You

I should expect miracles because God is still displaying His power among His people.

Turn to Jesus

Now that you know these things, God
will bless you for doing them.

—John 13:17

What do you do when you're having a bad day? You know, a day when your teacher is in a bad mood, your best friend is mad at you, you leave your lunch at home, you're coming down with a cold, and you drop your math book into a mud puddle. Do you skip home from school, hug your mom, and offer to help with dinner? Or do you slam the front door, stomp up the stairs, and flop down on your bed?

I know what most of us would do! And while it's perfectly fine to feel sorry for yourself, remember to turn to God when you're feeling down. He wants you to talk to Him about your problems. And He wants you to trust Him to handle them.

To you, things that go wrong are *problems*. To Jesus, things that go wrong are *possibilities*. That's why He wants you to talk to Him. You might think, *But Jesus already knows what my problems are!* That's true, but He wants you to get into the habit of turning to Him when things go wrong. And He also wants you to get into the habit of trusting Him.

The Bible says, "Give *all* your worries and cares to God, for he cares about you" (1 Peter 5:7, emphasis added). If something matters to us, it matters to Jesus.

Jesus never met a problem He couldn't solve. As long as the person with the problem did what Jesus asked, He was able to help them. And that's true today. That's why He encourages us to turn to Him whenever we're having a bad day or feeling sad or scared. He knows He is the answer to every one of our problems.

Remember, if something matters to you, it absolutely matters to Jesus.

▶ **Jesus, thank You that I can trust You with any problem in my life. I know that if I hand it over to You, You will take care of it, and You will take care of me.**

Take This with You

Everything that matters to me also matters to Jesus.

Safe in the Storm

When Jesus woke up, he rebuked the wind and
said to the waves, "Silence! Be still!" Suddenly the
wind stopped, and there was a great calm.

—Mark 4:39

Have you ever had a storm sneak up on you? One minute the sky is blue and the sun is shining. Suddenly, the gentle breeze turns into a forceful wind, and before you know it clouds have rolled in along with thunder and lightning.

Jesus's disciples once found themselves caught in a sudden storm on the Sea of Galilee. Jesus had been teaching all day, and when evening came, He told the disciples to take the boat to the other side of the sea. While Jesus was asleep in the boat, the sky grew black, the rain began to fall, and the wind stirred up the waves so much that they broke over the side of the boat. Even though Jesus was in the boat, the disciples panicked!

The frightened disciples woke Jesus up and asked, "Don't you care if we drown?" (Mark 4:38). If they had remembered that they could always trust Jesus, they might have taken a nap or played a game or read a book or simply enjoyed the wild weather! But they forgot. It's easy to forget things when you're worried!

Of course, all Jesus had to do to stop the storm was to tell the wind and the waves, "Silence! Be still!" (Mark 4:39). The storm stopped. Jesus had the power to stop the storm, and He also had the power to keep everyone on the boat safe in the storm.

Sometimes we'll have storms in our lives. We might have stormy days when we argue with our parents, get in fights with our friends, and feel like everything is going wrong. Often, these stormy days sneak up on us. We don't plan them. We don't wake up in the morning and say, "I think I'm going to have a really bad day today!" They just happen.

Instead of facing your stormy days with fear, face them the way Jesus wants you to face them—with faith. And remember that Jesus has promised He will always calm the storm.

▶ Jesus, I know I don't need to fear when You are near. Please be near me in every storm.

Take This with You

I can trust Jesus in every storm.

Give What You Have

Give freely and become more wealthy;
be stingy and lose everything.

—Proverbs 11:24

Let's say you are eager to start in on the meal in your lunch box, even though it isn't much. But then your friend asks to trade your fruit for his, and gives you not only a pear for your grapes but a nectarine too. Another friend trades you a turkey sandwich with lettuce, tomato, and mayo for your plain peanut butter sandwich, and throws in a chocolate chip cookie too! By being willing to give your friends what you could have kept for yourself, you received more than you gave in return!

Something way bigger than a lunchroom trade happened in the Bible. When Jesus fed the five thousand on the shores of Galilee, He didn't call up His favorite restaurant and say, "Hey, I have five thousand mouths to feed. Send Me your best fish and chips, with plenty of tartar sauce." Not even close! Instead, one of the disciples introduced Jesus to a little boy whose mom had packed his lunch box with some loaves of bread and a few fish. Back then, a *loaf of bread* was a small, dry wafer about the size of a mini-pancake. And by *fish*, the Bible meant a teeny, tiny sea creature about the size of a sardine.

The little boy had a little lunch. But what made that little lunch a big feast is what the boy did when Jesus asked for it.

The boy gave his lunch—all of it—to Jesus.

And then Jesus did something totally bizarre. He thanked God for the food!

Wait—*what?*

As the loaves and fish were passed around, people ate and ate and still there was more food. And when everyone had eaten their fill, twelve baskets were still overflowing with leftovers. Crazy!

No matter how small your gift is, Jesus will always use it. All of us are carrying around our little lunches—talents, abilities, even small allowances. When you give Jesus these things, He uses them in amazing ways to bless others, and you'll get to enjoy a yummy feast as well as the leftovers.

▶ **Jesus, teach me to trust You with what I have. I know that as I give, You will bless others.**

Take This with You

Give generously to God, and He will
bless you and those around you.

Followers

Come, follow me, and I will show you how
to fish for people!

—Mark 1:17

Keeping chickens is really popular right now—in the city as well as out in the country. You probably know someone who has chickens. Maybe your own family raises chickens. And if you're familiar with chickens, you're probably familiar with the term *pecking order*.

In the pecking order, you have one chicken in charge of the rest. This "top" chicken gets all the good stuff—the best spot on the roost at night, first pick of the treats, the best nesting box. When other chickens try to challenge the top bird, they get pecked. The sooner they catch on and learn to follow the leader, the fewer pecks they get. It might sound mean, but chickens need a pecking order. Every flock needs a leader.

Did you know God has built a pecking order into our lives? You follow your parents or your teachers or other leaders. And you follow God. From the time you're born, the first lesson Jesus wants you to learn is not how to lead but how to follow.

The disciples spent three years following Jesus around

and learning how to lead from Him. And most of them then went on to become the first leaders of the early church. They had to learn how to follow before they could lead.

Even Jesus followed the rule of leading by following first:

- He followed His *parents*: "Then he returned to Nazareth with [his parents] and was obedient to them" (Luke 2:51).

- He followed His *Father* (God): "For I have come down from heaven to do the will of God who sent me, not to do my own will" (John 6:38).

- He followed the *Holy Spirit*: "Jesus, full of the Holy Spirit, returned from the Jordan River. He was led by the Spirit in the wilderness" (Luke 4:1).

First, you learn how to follow. Then you learn how to lead. It's best to follow the lead of Jesus because He is the ultimate leader.

▶ **Jesus, teach me what it means to be a faithful follower of You.**

Take This with You

When I learn how to follow, I also learn how to lead.

What Excites Jesus

And the man jumped up, grabbed his mat,
and walked out through the stunned onlookers.
They were all amazed and praised God, exclaiming,
"We've never seen anything like this before!"

—Mark 2:12

What gets you excited? Is it waking up to a big snowfall and the promise of a day spent sledding or snowboarding, building a snowman, and drinking hot chocolate? Does the countdown to Christmas or your birthday get you excited? Maybe winning a sporting event or game gets you really pumped up.

Did you know there's one thing that gets Jesus super excited? It's seeing our faith. When Jesus sees us believing in Him and putting our trust in Him, He can't help but be thrilled. You see this happen in the Bible when Jesus healed people. While the healing was a really big deal—imagine being blind and able to see again or stuck in a wheelchair and suddenly able to walk again—the bigger deal to Jesus was seeing people grow in their faith.

The people being healed—and those around them— were excited about their physical healing, but Jesus was more excited about their spiritual healing. They were pumped about what was happening here on earth, but Jesus was even more pumped about what was going to happen in heaven.

Being blind or unable to walk is nothing compared to sin. Those are temporary problems. Sin is an eternal—or forever—problem. If your sins have been forgiven, you have a place in heaven. And when Jesus sees you're going to be in heaven one day, He gets excited!

▶ **Jesus, thank You for forgiving my sins and giving me a place in heaven. Help me to tell others about You so they can have a place in heaven too.**

Take This with You

The thing that brings Jesus the most excitement is when I have faith in Him.

I Can See!

"I don't know whether he is a sinner," the man replied.
"But I do know this: I was blind, and now I can see!"

—John 9:25

If you've ever stumbled around in the dark until you found a light switch, you know a little what it's like to be blind. Not completely, of course, but you can imagine it. And then when you turn on the light—wow! You can see everything!

People who don't know Jesus are living in the darkness. You could have perfect 20/20 vision. You could read the letters on the teeniest, tiniest line on the eye chart at the doctor's office. But without Jesus, you're as blind as a bat. That's because not only do you have eyes in your head, but you also have eyes in your heart.

Eyes in your heart? That sounds pretty weird, doesn't it? But it's true. The eyes in your heart are your spiritual eyes, and you use them to do things like see right from wrong. You also use them to see God and focus on Him.

The Bible tells the story of a man who was blind from birth. He had never, ever been able to see. Anything. Ever!

Jesus did something pretty crazy for this man. He spit on the ground, making mud with His own saliva, and washed the man's eyes with that mixture. And guess what happened? After the man washed the mud out with water, he could see! Not only could he see the trees and the people and the sky and the clouds around him, he could also see Jesus. And he believed in Jesus.

When we choose to open our eyes and do as God asks—like the blind man washing the mud out of his eyes—we see Jesus. And that's the brightest light of all!

▶ **Jesus, please shine Your light in my heart so I may see You.**

Take This with You

Jesus is the light of the world. With Him,
I am never in darkness.

Watching Over You

He will order his angels to protect and guard you.

—Luke 4:10

Have you ever seen a really small child trying new things at the playground?

"Watch me!" the little person exclaims. "Watch me climb the stairs! Watch me slide! Watch me swing!"

Watch me! We all have a need to be watched. But I'm not talking about being watched like a toddler or preschooler is watched. I'm talking about a different kind of watching—a spiritual watching.

When God created the world and looked over "all he had made," He saw that it was "very good!" (Genesis 1:31). Besides plants and animals and people, "all he had made" includes angels. You can't see angels here on earth, but they do exist. They're *spiritual* beings, and one of their jobs is to protect us.

Just as you can be "an angel" to a tiny toddler—catching her at the bottom of the slide or pushing her on the swings— God's angels are always there to help you. You may not be able to see them, but God promises they are there. Angels aren't fairies or make-believe characters. They are real—as real as you and me and the God we all serve. And it's so comforting to know they are protecting us!

Beyond that, you have God Himself guarding and protecting you. Talk about being well cared for!

As you travel through the playground of life, God's angels—as well as God Himself—are there caring for you and protecting you. They're watching you always!

▶ **Jesus, thank You for sending angels to protect me. Help me to trust You always.**

Take This with You

God sends His angels to watch over me.

Growing God's Garden

*Other seeds fell on fertile soil, and they produced
a crop that was thirty, sixty, and even a hundred
times as much as had been planted!*

—Matthew 13:8

If you've ever planted a garden at home or grown some seeds at school, you know you can have the perfect seed and just the right amount of sunlight and water, but that doesn't mean your seed will sprout and your plant will grow. You need the right soil! If you plant your seed in the rocks or in soil that's been taken over by weeds, that little seed doesn't have a chance of growing. But if the soil is good, the plant can put down healthy roots and grow strong.

The story Jesus tells in Matthew 13:1-9 is all about the soil. Who the farmer—the person who scatters the seed—is doesn't matter. The type of seed doesn't matter. The thing that matters is the soil. Too rocky, too weedy, too sandy—the plant won't grow. But when the seed falls on *good* soil, it will grow.

Do you know how someone who doesn't believe in Jesus can become a Christian? By having the seed of God's Word planted in his or her heart.

And did you know you can have a part in growing God's garden? You can be the farmer who plants the seed!

The seed is God's Word—the incredible message that Jesus loves you and that He died on the cross to save you from your sin and give you eternal life.

The soil is the heart of the person hearing God's message.

And the farmer is you! You can be the one to tell others about Jesus. You can sow the seeds of God's Word in the soil of another person's life.

The great thing about this garden is that God does the work. He's the one who makes it grow. We don't have to feel like a failure if we tell a friend about Jesus and she doesn't believe.

Our job is to sow. God's job is to grow.

We plant seeds of God's Word when we show kindness to others, tell them how Jesus helps us, or invite them to a fun church activity. Growing God's garden can be easy—and fun!

▶ **Jesus, help me to be brave and tell my friends about You.**

Take This with You

I do my job. Jesus will do His.

A Fair Teacher

*Oh, how generous and gracious our Lord was! He filled
me with the faith and love that come from Christ Jesus.*

—1 Timothy 1:14

What would you think of a teacher who promised her
class candy if they got the extra credit problems correct on a test? That would be fair, right?

But let's say the test has ten extra credit problems, and
you got all ten of them right. The kid sitting next to you got
only one extra credit problem right. *I'm going to get way more
candy*, you think...until the teacher hands you ten pieces of
candy and also counts out ten pieces for the kid next to you.

Hey, that's not fair! you think. *I deserve more candy than he
does! After all, I got nine more problems right.*

If we're looking at the teacher the way we look at God,
we have to realize the teacher *is* being fair. She promised
her students candy for correct answers, and she was fair
because she kept her promise. Beyond that, she was generous. God is the same way. There's no rule saying He has to
give us anything—but He gives to us anyway. That's called
grace.

God doesn't have to invite anyone to be a part of His

family. He doesn't have to bless anyone with gifts. He doesn't have to answer our prayers. But He does those things because He loves us and because He's fair and just. He's gracious and generous.

When we compare what we have to what someone else has, we risk being ungrateful to God. That's why we shouldn't compare. God has His reasons for giving what He does, when He does. Just remember—God is always generous, and He's always fair.

▶ Jesus, give me a heart that is a reflection of Your own heart. Thank You for being fair—and generous.

Take This with You

God is fair and generous all the time.

21

A Good Neighbor

Love the LORD your God with all your heart,
all your soul, all your strength, and all your
mind... Love your neighbor as yourself.

—Luke 10:27

Do you know all your neighbors? You might know the family next door really well, but the people across the street are a total mystery. Or maybe you just moved in and the people who live in the house on one side of you welcomed your family with cookies, but you've never seen the people who live on the other side.

In the Bible, Jesus tells us we are supposed to love God and love our neighbor. Loving God makes sense. But what about our neighbor? Who exactly is your neighbor? Is it the family who delivered the cookies? Is it the old man who rarely leaves his house? Is it the guy you see wandering down your street looking for cans and bottles on recycling day?

Actually, *everyone* is your neighbor! God brings different people into all of our lives at different times. And while I wouldn't recommend wandering the streets in search of people to talk to, I would recommend thinking of everyone you meet as your neighbor. The kids in your class at school are your neighbors. Your teammates and coaches at soccer are your neighbors—and so are the players on the other team. The people you see at the grocery store or ice-cream shop are your neighbors. And what does Jesus say we should do for our neighbors? *Love your neighbor as yourself.*

If you're feeling sad, it helps if a friend hangs out with you, doesn't it? So start noticing how the people around you are doing. Share a smile with them. Ask, "How are you doing today?" Give them a compliment. You don't have to do big things to be a good neighbor. It's the little things that really count. God's love in your heart will help you be a good neighbor.

▶ **Jesus, sometimes it's tempting to not talk to people. Help me to be a good neighbor to everyone around me.**

Take This with You

God commands me to love my neighbor as myself.

22

Every Instrument Counts

All of you together are Christ's body,
and each of you is a part of it.

—1 Corinthians 12:27

If you've ever played an instrument in a band or sung in a choir, you know it's important to work with the other musicians. The drummer can't just do her own thing, and even the best singer can't just sing whatever he wants. Everyone needs to work together as a group. And even if you're a total beginner on the flute or you're in the church musical for the first time, you still have an important part to play.

It's the same way for those who believe in Jesus. We all have a part to play, and we all need to follow God's direction. Some instruments are louder than others and some singers have more solos, but it's not how loud you play or how often you sing that matters to Jesus. It's what you do with your instrument or voice that matters to Him.

Everyone in this world is born into a different family and into a different situation. But God has given everyone their own unique talents and abilities. And even though you might feel like everyone else has more talent than you do, remember that there are no unimportant instruments in God's orchestra. None!

All Jesus asks us to do is to play our part and do our best. He doesn't expect everyone to sound exactly the same. But He does expect that we will give it our best effort. What's really nice to know is that He will never, ever compare you to someone else. He doesn't choose first chair (or last chair!) Christians. We're all in this together. He's only going to compare you with *you*. So play your heart out!

▶ **Jesus, teach me to give my best effort with the talents You've given me. Help me to use them wisely and share them freely.**

Take This with You

Jesus doesn't look at what I have.
He only looks at what I do with what I have.

23

It's All God's Stuff

When God's people are in need, be ready to help them.

—Romans 12:13

Did you know you are one of the richest people in the world? This might sound a little crazy if you have a parent who's looking for a job or your family drives really old cars or your house is totally not a mansion. But it's true. People only need three things to live: shelter, food, and clothing. If you have a roof over your head and food in your cupboards and you're wearing clothes, you have more than a lot of people have.

There are other ways of measuring how much you have too. Do you have friends? Do you go to school and church? Are you involved in any clubs or activities? Those things also make you rich—rich on the inside.

One of the richest men in the world was once asked, "How much money is enough?"

The rich man replied, "Just a little bit more. Just a little bit more."

That kind of thinking is really common in our world today. We might be talking about food or electronics or clothes or even having fun with our friends. We have plenty right now, but we always want just a little bit more.

In the Bible, Jesus warns us to "Guard against every kind of greed" (Luke 12:15) or, in other words, to be in control of what you want.

The way to avoid always wanting more is to change the way you think about your stuff. Most people think what they have is *theirs*. But if you understand that everything you have comes from God and also belongs to God, you'll think about your stuff completely differently. You'll want to share more.

You can share your allowance by giving to your church. You can share your friends by introducing them to someone who seems lonely. You can share your home and your belongings by inviting people over. Share what you have—and especially share God's love!

Jesus, thank You for meeting my needs. Please help me give to those who need what I have.

Take This with You

Everything I have comes from God.
He shares with me so I can share with others.

24

Planning Ahead

Each of us will give a personal account to God.

—Romans 14:12

If your family has a super busy week coming up, do your parents do some things to plan ahead? Your mom might write out a meal plan for the week and stock up on groceries and snacks like fruit and energy bars. Or your dad gets all the laundry done on the weekend so everyone has clean clothes to wear all week. You might also plan ahead. You could get your homework done early or lay out your clothes and pack your schoolbag the night before.

God wants us to be smart with how we use our time. He wants us to use our today to get ready for tomorrow. And I'm not just talking about the *actual* today—like today is Wednesday and tomorrow is Thursday. When God talks about *today* and *tomorrow*, He means life on this earth (today) and life in heaven (tomorrow). He wants everything we do today to be planning ahead for tomorrow.

The greatest example of planning ahead is the life of Jesus. He spent His thirty-three years on earth serving God and teaching about Him to prepare us for heaven. And then

He did the ultimate act of planning ahead—He died on the cross and was raised from the dead so we could all have a tomorrow. And not just any tomorrow! If we believe in Him, our tomorrow will be spent living with Him in heaven.

So when you plan ahead, don't just pack your schoolbag for the next day. Pack your mind and your heart full of God's Word. Use your today to get ready for tomorrow!

▶ **Jesus, please help me to use my time wisely and plan ahead so my tomorrow is all You have promised it will be.**

Take This with You

Jesus wants me to use my today
to prepare for tomorrow.

25

Lost and Found

When he arrives, he will call together his
friends and neighbors, saying, "Rejoice with
me because I have found my lost sheep."

—Luke 15:6

Have you ever had to go digging through the lost-and-found box for something you misplaced? Depending on where you are, it can be quite the search! Sometimes everything in the box is so icky and grungy that you sort of don't *want* to find the jacket or water bottle or book you lost.

Did you know God digs through the lost and found, searching for us? It doesn't matter if we're sitting on top or buried deep in the bottom of the bin. He is going to keep digging and searching until He finds us! Now, we're not *really* in a lost-and-found box, of course. But when we wander away from God and start making choices that aren't the choices He wants us to make, He always brings us back to Him.

The Bible tells of a shepherd who had ninety-nine sheep that were in the field and one that was lost. The shepherd didn't say, "Oh, well. I have a lot of sheep anyway. That one lost sheep doesn't matter. I'm going to stay in my field and take a nap." No, he went in search of that one lost sheep. And when he found it, the shepherd rejoiced.

It's the same way with Jesus and us. Lost people matter to Jesus. He wants all of us to be a part of His family, and when someone is lost and separated from Him, He will always do His best to find that person and bring them back to Him.

▶ **Jesus, thank You that we are so valuable to You and that You will always search for us when we are lost.**

Take This with You

Because lost people matter to Jesus, they should matter to me.

26

The Best Invitation

What a blessing it will be to attend a
banquet in the Kingdom of God!

—Luke 14:15

What if you received an invitation like this?

> You're invited to my birthday party! A trip to Disneyland, followed by a day of playing on the beach in Hawaii, followed by a snow trip to the mountains. All your favorite foods will be served, and we'll pay for everything. We even provide the birthday present!

Would you accept that invitation? Definitely! But what if you arrived at Disneyland, ready for the party to start, and you were the only guest? Other friends were invited, but they all had something else to do. One had to give his dog a bath. Another decided she wanted to get a little more sleep. And yet another decided to go grocery shopping with his parents.

Those are some pretty crazy excuses, aren't they? How could bathing your dog, getting more sleep, or going grocery shopping be better than the most awesome birthday party ever? But Jesus tells us some people are like that. They'll turn down an invitation to the most amazing thing ever—being part of the kingdom of God and spending eternity in heaven—because they think they have something better to do.

Jesus is the host of the big party, and He invites everyone to be a part of His kingdom and to be one of His special guests. There's really *no* legitimate reason to say no to His invitation. Not only will you miss out on a relationship with God, but you'll also never experience the wonder of heaven.

When you say yes to Jesus's invitation to join His family, you'll have a blast sitting at the table of the Creator of the universe, the King of kings and the Lord of lords, and enjoying the celebration forever!

▶ **Thank You, Jesus, that You've invited me to Your party. Help me to always be ready to say yes to Your every invitation.**

Take This with You

God honors me with the invitation
to be a part of His family.

27

Grace

*Those who exalt themselves will be humbled, and
those who humble themselves will be exalted.*

—Luke 18:14

Do you ever look at kids who don't go to church and think you're better than they are, because you do go to church? Do you ever look at kids who use bad words and think you're better than they are, because you don't? Do you ever look at someone who always acts mean or bullies others and think you're better than they are, because you don't?

It can be easy to look down on others, especially if you see them behaving in a way you know you're not supposed to behave. But Jesus tells us that when we look up to God, we will not be tempted to look down on others.

All of us make mistakes. None of us is perfect. We all need God's love and forgiveness. We all need His grace.

God understands—and wants all of us to understand—that everyone is a sinner. Nobody is perfect. He wants us to see ourselves correctly. And He wants us to see Him correctly. When you see God—and yourself—correctly, you'll understand that only God is perfect and no one else is.

When you're tempted to compare yourself to others and

look down on them, first look up to God. Ask Him to help you pray for the people you're looking down on and to see them as He sees them. Of course, this doesn't mean you need to act like them. Not at all! But it can help you realize that we are all sinners who need God's grace. We're all in this together.

▶ **Jesus, I confess that I'm a sinner in need of grace. Please forgive me for thinking I'm better than someone else, and help me to see You—and myself—more clearly.**

Take This with You

None of us is too good or not good enough. God's grace is available to every one of us!

28

Welcome Back

We had to celebrate this happy day. For your
brother was dead and has come back to
life! He was lost, but now he is found!

—Luke 15:32

Pretend your little brother asked for some money from your dad. But instead of saving it, he ran to the store a mile from your house to buy some ice cream without telling anyone where he was going. And he was gone a long time. Do you think your dad would be mad that your brother used the money for ice cream? Probably. Do you think he would be upset that he ran away? Yes—and worried too! Do you think he would throw a party for your brother when he finally got back home? Um...probably not.

This same kind of situation happened in the Bible. You might remember the parable of the prodigal son. When the son who took the money and wasn't responsible and left home decided to come back, the father threw a big party to celebrate his return. Some people might think this seems kind of unfair. After all, the son took his dad's money! *And* he ran away!

But we should be happy about this story because it shows

us just how much God loves us. No matter what you've done wrong and no matter how far away from God you've run, His door is always open and His message is always, "Welcome home! Let's have a party to celebrate!" Everyone—no matter who they are, where they are, or what they've done—has a Father who loves them.

When you're feeling sad or you're sick or you've gotten hurt—even when you've made mistakes—where do you want to be? Home, right? All of us have a need to be safe at home when things aren't going well. God understands this. That's why He will always be there for you, welcoming you back home with open arms and a loving heart.

▶ **Jesus, thank You for welcoming me back home whenever I have done anything wrong or run away from You.**

Take This with You

God's heart is always open to welcome me back home.

29

You Never Know

But those who obey God's word truly show how
completely they love him. That is how we know
we are living in him. Those who say they live
in God should live their lives as Jesus did.

—1 John 2:5-6

There was once a poor Italian violin maker. He made his violins from pieces of wood that he found washed up on the shores of a dirty harbor. The violin maker took these ruined pieces of wood to his shop, where he would create instruments of rare beauty. Later, it was discovered that it was the waterlogged wood that allowed the most amazing sounds ever heard to come out of his violins.

From wood that nobody wanted, the Italian violin maker—Antonio Stradivari—created violins that now everybody wants. No violin sounds as incredible as a Stradivarius violin.

Just as the poor violin maker transformed trash into treasure, God can transform us into what we were truly meant to be. And if you already believe in God, it's important to remember that you never know who else might end up believing in Him. The boy who is a bully on the playground or the girl who talks back to the teacher might someday become a follower of Jesus.

At some point, God determines who follows Him. And He does this by asking one question: *Who is your Father?* If you say God is your Father and Jesus is your Savior, you're a part of God's family. And you just never know who else you might see in heaven someday! You never know who could become a part of God's family.

▶ Jesus, thank You for forgiving my sins and turning me into Your treasure.

Take This with You

God's job is to turn trash into treasure and sinners into saints.

30

Look Ahead

Not everyone who calls out to me, "Lord! Lord!"
will enter the Kingdom of Heaven. Only those who
actually do the will of my Father in heaven will enter.

—Matthew 7:21

Do you remember learning to ride a bike? You were so focused on putting your feet on the pedals and gripping the handlebars and keeping your balance that you sometimes forgot to look where you were going. And then you ran into something!

Just like we need to see where we're going when we're riding a bike, we need to see where we're going in life. Jesus talks about this in the Bible when He talks about living our lives with our eyes focused on the future. He knew life on earth was just a tiny little *blip* compared to the eternity we will spend in heaven.

I heard about a Sunday school teacher who was telling his class the story of the rich man and Lazarus. The rich man had everything he needed on this earth but didn't understand that he needed to follow God. Lazarus, though he was poor, had a relationship with Jesus.

The teacher pointed out how one man was rich and one

man was poor while they were on this earth. After they died, he explained, one man went to be with God and one man went to live without God. After he finished the lesson, the teacher said, "Who would you rather be? The rich man or Lazarus?" One quick-thinking kid raised his hand and said, "I'd like to be the rich man while I'm alive and Lazarus when I'm dead."

That sounds great, doesn't it? Well, it doesn't really work that way! You can't live however you want to and only think about Jesus and heaven at the very last minute. You need to look ahead. Begin now to live for God, look to God, and listen to God, for that is the only life that will matter both today and tomorrow.

▶ **Jesus, help me to live my life looking ahead and living for You.**

Take This with You

My decisions today determine what my tomorrow will be like.

31

See Yourself Clearly

Do not judge others, and you will not be judged. For you
will be treated as you treat others. The standard you use
in judging is the standard by which you will be judged.

—**Matthew 7:1-2**

Have you ever looked at someone and thought, *That person would make a good friend*? And have you ever looked at another person and thought, *That person doesn't seem very much like me. We probably won't ever be friends*. Sometimes you're right, and sometimes you're wrong. It's not always the best choice to assume stuff about people based on what they look like on the outside.

Of course, once you get to know a person and see how they act, you can get a better idea of what kind of friend that person will be. The problem is when we care more about what a person looks like on the outside than what they look like on the inside.

If you want to see what you look like, you look in a mirror. If you want to see what someone else looks like, you look out the window. Jesus says we need to spend more time looking in the mirror than we spend looking out the window. This doesn't mean you totally focus on yourself and don't think about other people. It does mean you need to make sure you are acting the way Jesus wants you to act before judging other people.

If you think someone is being mean or leaving you out, first look in the mirror to make sure you're being kind and including others. Look in the mirror before you look out the window.

If someone is doing something wrong—like bullying someone else—it's okay to stand up for the person being bullied or say, "Hey, you need to stop doing that!" Not being judgmental *doesn't* mean ignoring things that are wrong. Ultimately, though, it's God's job to judge. It's our job to see ourselves clearly as we love God and love others.

> Jesus, teach me to look in the mirror and see myself clearly. Make me aware of how I'm treating others and how I am living the way You want me to live.

Take This with You

I need to spend more time looking in the mirror than looking out the window.

32

Sharing Secrets

When you pray, go away by yourself, shut the door
behind you, and pray to your Father in private. Then
your Father, who sees everything, will reward you.

—Matthew 6:6

You've shared a secret with a friend, haven't you? Think about where you've shared that secret. Is it better to share it in a crowded room with a lot of other people right by you, or is it better to share it in private? If you're sharing something you want only your friend to hear, it's better to share in private, isn't it?

The best person to share secrets with is God. And the best place to share them with Him is in private. When Jesus's disciples were trying to figure out how to pray, the first thing Jesus told them was *where* they should pray. He didn't say, "These are the magic words you should say when you pray" or "Your prayer should last exactly one minute." Nope, the first thing He said was to pray in private.

Jesus said this because prayer is a conversation between you and God. You don't pray to get attention or to look like a really good Christian or to get stuff from God. The main point of praying is to get closer to God and to get to know Him better. It's like talking to a friend so you can get to know her better. And the best place to do that is where it's just you and your friend—at one of your houses, in the backyard, at the park.

You don't have to talk a lot when you pray. Jesus says it's not how *much* you say to God that causes Him to hear your prayers, but *how* you talk to Him that gets His attention. Even if you just say, "God, I'm here to hang out with You" and then just sit there and think about how awesome He is, that totally works! Prayer is all about spending time with God, and the more you do it, the easier it becomes.

▶ **Jesus, help me to get to know You and spend time with You in prayer.**

Take This with You

No matter where you are,
you can share secrets with God.

33

Focus on the Father

Give thanks for everything to God the Father
in the name of our Lord Jesus Christ.

—Ephesians 5:20

Have you ever prayed a prayer that seemed more like a birthday or Christmas wish list? Lots of "I want..." and "Please give me..." and not much listening to God? It's easy to get into the habit of praying this way because you can't actually hear God like you would hear your friend or your mom. But part of praying is listening to God. No matter if you hear Him in your heart or just get a feeling, He's there!

Listening to God is an important part of praying because the number one thing about prayer is that it's not to get God to do what *you* want. It's to get God to do what *He* wants. It's all about God.

It's not easy to put what God wants above what we want—especially when we don't know what God wants! Can you imagine writing out your birthday list and, instead of writing down that game or those shoes you really want, writing down, "Whatever you want me to have" or "Whatever you think would be best for me"? No way! But God is different from your great-grandma Lucy who sends you those crazy hand-knit sweaters. He's going to give you things that are good for you and that you will appreciate.

The best prayer you can ever pray for anyone, in any situation, in any place, is the prayer, "Your will be done." Do you know why? Because God's will is always the best and right thing to pray for.

If you're not used to praying very much, try to take just a few minutes each day to talk to God. Focus on who He is, where He lives, and what He wants. Then say, "Your will be done" and watch as He changes your life.

▶ **Jesus, help me to remember that it's not all about me. Help me to remember that it's actually all about You!**

Take This with You

Prayer is not about me getting what I want but God getting what He wants.

34

Why We Pray

*Praise God, who did not ignore my prayer or
withdraw his unfailing love from me.*

—Psalm 66:20

Have you ever tried and tried to understand something in your math or science book—and even had one of your parents try to explain it to you—but you only really understood when you asked your teacher? Life can be like that really hard-to-understand problem or idea. And sometimes God is the only one who can explain it to us. That's part of why it's so important to pray.

We pray because we have problems that only God can solve, questions that only God can answer, and needs that only God can meet. As we spend more time with God in prayer, we can be confident that He really hears our prayers. I know it's hard to imagine Him hearing your prayer when hundreds of thousands of people are talking to Him all at the same time, but He does!

A big part of prayer is learning to be thankful for all God has given us. While it's fine to ask God to meet our needs, we also need to focus on everything we *do* have and all the awesome stuff God is doing in our lives. The more thankful you are, the more you realize how many things you have to be thankful for. It's really cool how this works!

Something that can mess up our praying is sin we haven't confessed to God. Psalm 66:18 says, "If I had not confessed the sin in my heart, the Lord would not have listened." If we want God to hear our prayers, we need to ask Him to forgive our sins and to help us obey Him.

The more you talk to God and listen to what He says, the better you will understand Him. That's why we pray!

▶ **Jesus, thank You that I can always turn to You when I have questions or don't understand something. Help me to be thankful and to obey You.**

Take This with You

Sometimes God is the only one who can explain things to me.

35

Treasures

Don't store up treasures here on earth.

—Matthew 6:19

Have you ever done a treasure hunt? You start out with a clue and you go from place to place, looking for the next clue and the next until you finally discover the treasure at the end. And discovering that treasure is the most important part of the treasure hunt!

Let's say the treasure at the end was ice-cream sundaes. What if everyone participating in the treasure hunt decided to save their ice-cream sundaes instead of eating them? The ice cream would melt, the whipped cream would get all runny, the sprinkles would get all gross, and you'd never eat it.

Treasures are awesome, but only if we do something with them. That's why God warns us not to store them up. Now, it's not like you have an expensive car or a million dollars or a bunch of valuable jewels. But God has given you other kinds of treasure—nice friends, a talent for music or sports, even the ability to read quickly.

Jesus doesn't want you to become obsessed with your treasures. It doesn't matter to Him how many friends came to your birthday party or how many baskets you can make in a row. It *does* matter how you use your treasures, though.

You can form a clique with all your friends, or you can reach out to others. You can use your musical talent only for yourself, or you can bless others with it. You can use your ability to do well in school just to get great grades, or you can help others who are struggling to learn.

Jesus doesn't want your treasures. They already belong to Him. Jesus wants your heart. When you give your treasures to Jesus, you give Him your heart. And He will use them to bless both you and others.

▶ Jesus, all my treasures come from You. Help me to use them to bless others.

Take This with You

The most important part of a treasure is what I do with it.

36

A Friendship Coach

Two people are better off than one,
for they can help each other succeed. If one
person falls, one can reach out and help.

—Ecclesiastes 4:9-10

Besides your relationship with God and your relationship with your family, friendships are the most important relationships in your life. Some people have a whole bunch of friends. Others have just a few close friends. Making friends comes easily to some people. Others take their time making friends. Sometimes friends move away or a friendship just changes.

When friendships change or when you feel like you don't have many friends—like when you move to a new school or start a new activity—you can feel sad and lonely. At times like this turn to God, because He's the one who created friendship.

You can think of God as your friendship coach. If you're struggling to find good friends who love God, ask Him to bring those people into your life. If you have friends who aren't a very good influence on you, ask God to help you with that. Maybe God has some other friends—*better* friends—in mind for you.

The Bible tells us we weren't created to live alone and do things by ourselves. God says "two people are better off than one" (Ecclesiastes 4:9) and that friends should be able to help each other.

If you're struggling with your friendships, remember that Jesus is the ultimate friendship coach and you can go to Him with your friendship problems. After all, He's your very best friend forever.

▶ **Jesus, thank You for creating friendship. Please help me to find good friends.**

Take This with You

Friends are important, and God can help me make the best kind of friends.

37

Gossip Isn't Good

A troublemaker plants seeds of strife;
gossip separates the best of friends.

—Proverbs 16:28

Once you've found good friends, it's important to keep them. The Bible talks a lot about how we should treat other people, including how to talk to them—what kind of words should come out of our mouths and what kind of words shouldn't.

God warns us about the danger of gossip—spreading stuff about other people that either isn't true or that's not our business to share. Making up something about someone else and spreading that around is gossip. So is sharing what someone told you in private. So is telling other people stuff you probably aren't supposed to know—like something you overheard your parents or teachers saying.

Gossip might get you a lot of attention, especially if you get a reputation as the person who always has the latest "news" and knows what's going on. But spreading gossip gets you the *wrong* kind of attention. People won't trust you. And gossip is incredibly hurtful. It can destroy friendships and make things really awful between people—even people who used to be best friends.

If you believe in Jesus, you need to know that gossip has no place in a Christian's life. And it's important to know gossip when you see it. If something isn't true, it's gossip. If it's shared to make someone look bad or to hurt someone, it's gossip. If it's whispered or said along with something like, "Don't tell anyone this…" or "I probably shouldn't say this…" it's gossip.

The best way to respond when someone gossips to you is to say, "Hey, I don't really want to hear this. That's gossip. Let's talk about something else." The more you respond this way, the less gossip people will share with you. And that's a good thing! Jesus wants us to love each other. We can show that love by speaking good words, not words of gossip.

▶ **Jesus, please help the words that come out of my mouth to be true and kind and friendship-building, not words of gossip that are friendship-destroying.**

Take This with You

My friendships will be stronger
if I don't gossip and don't listen to gossip.

38

Love One Another

Your love for one another will prove to the
world that you are my disciples.

—John 13:35

If you have brothers and sisters, you probably know you can love people without always liking them. When you fight and argue with someone, you're not exactly liking them right then. But after you've worked through the problem and forgiven each other, you realize you still love that person. Actually, the fact that you have worked things out and made them better shows that you love your brother or your sister. Love is like that!

Jesus told His disciples—who were like family to each other—to love each other: "So now I am giving you a new commandment: Love each other. Just as I have loved you, you should love each other. Your love for one another will prove to the world that you are my disciples" (John 13:34-35).

Liking someone and loving someone are actually different things. Jesus never commanded us to like our enemies. That's because liking someone is a feeling, not a choice.

Loving, though, is a choice. It's an action—something you do. You don't have to like someone to love them.

Jesus tells us we're supposed to love each other the way He has loved us. That's pretty intense love because He showed us His love by dying on the cross for our sins! Now, you don't have to die on the cross for someone, but you do have to love them. And that means putting them first and being kind even when you don't feel like it.

For three years, Jesus put His disciples first—washing their feet, saving them from a storm, patiently teaching them. He taught them by example what it looked like to love each other. And He expects us to do the same. That's how others will know about His love.

▶ **Jesus, teach me to love others, even when I might not always like them.**

Take This with You

I don't have to like someone to love them, but I do need to choose loving actions.

What's Most Important

Seek the Kingdom of God above all else, and live
righteously, and he will give you everything you need.

—Matthew 6:33

What's more important—your math or spelling homework? Your friend's slumber party or your sister's choir concert? Your basketball practice or your play rehearsal? Sometimes you have to make choices in your life. A lot of the time, the things you're choosing between are both good things, but you need to choose the best thing. Fortunately, your parents can help you make the choice. And God will always help you see what's most important.

Jesus gives some great advice about choosing the most important thing when He tells us to seek the kingdom of God. If you make your most important thing what God thinks is most important, everything will work out just right. So what do you need to do? Figure out what's most important to Jesus!

You figure out what's most important to Jesus by getting to know Him. Read His words in your Bible. Pray and listen to Him. Learn about Him in Sunday school and church. Getting to know Jesus is the most important thing of all!

Once you decide that whatever Jesus wants in your life is the same thing you want in your life, you've solved the problem of how to choose what's most important. In every decision you make, either *you* will decide to do what you want to do or you will decide to do what *God* wants you to do. The closer you are to God, the more you'll choose to do what He wants you to do. And that is what's most important!

▶ **Jesus, please help me to know what is important to You. Give me the desire to do what matters most to You.**

Take This with You

Once I understand what is important to God,
I will understand what should be important to me.

40

Free!

Is anyone thirsty? Come and drink—even if you have no
money! Come, take your choice of wine or milk—it's all free!

—Isaiah 55:1

An airline once made a mistake on their website. They
advertised seats on a flight from Canada to Greece
for $39. That's really cheap for plane tickets! The price of the
tickets was supposed to be $3900, but the person putting
the ad on the website left off two zeros. Customers bought
two thousand tickets, and the mistake cost the airline $7.7
million. Oops!

The airline made a big mistake. Somebody messed up. I
don't know if that person lost his job, but his boss probably
didn't say, "No big deal. Don't worry about it."

One of the most awesome things about Jesus is that,
even when we mess up, we don't lose our place in His family. We don't have to pay Him back for our mistakes. We
don't have to earn His approval or love back because He
gives us His love for free. That's an even better deal than a
$39 plane ticket!

Jesus paid for all the mistakes anyone would ever make
when He died for us on the cross and set us free. Talk about

generous! And because Jesus is so generous to us, He expects us to be generous to others. We are worthy of His time, attention, and love—so others should be worthy of our time, attention, and love.

Anybody—no matter who they are or what they've done—can become a part of the family of God. We don't need to earn our way there or pay God back for the mistakes we've made. His grace and love are free. Our job is to accept them and enjoy the journey!

▶ **Jesus, teach me to accept Your love and to see others the way You see them—as being worthy of time, attention, and love.**

Take This with You

God's grace and love for me are free.
All I need to do is accept them.

41

Losers Who Win

If you cling to your life, you will lose it; but if you give up your life for me, you will find it.

—Matthew 10:39

I just love losing!"

Have you ever heard anyone say that? Probably not! Most people don't go into something trying to lose. Whether it's a baseball game or a dance competition, the competitors practice and practice and then practice some more to *win*.

Jesus said some totally crazy things about losing. In fact, He encourages us to lose! If finding Him and living for Him means losing our power or our stuff or our popularity, then Jesus is all for losing. Only when we lose ourselves do we find what really matters in life.

The Bible tells the story of a rich young ruler who had it all—money, power, you name it. He asked Jesus what he needed to do to have eternal life. Jesus told him he needed to give all he had to the poor. *Then* he would have treasure in heaven. "If you want God in your heart," Jesus said, "you've got to give your heart to God."

Guess what? The rich man couldn't do it. I think that, in many ways, he really wanted to, but in the end he just couldn't do it. And because he couldn't lose, he also couldn't win. If he'd said, "Sure, Jesus! Here are all my things. Let's go give them to the poor!" he would have been a winner.

God doesn't usually ask us to sell everything we have. But He might ask us to lose a friendship that isn't good for us, or He might ask us to give some of our stuff to those who don't have much. When you start surrendering everything to Jesus, God will make you into the biggest winner.

▶ Jesus, everything I have belongs to You. I surrender all I have to You.

Take This with You

If you want God in your heart,
you need to give your heart to God.

42

Confessions

But if we confess our sins to him, he is faithful and just to forgive us our sins and to cleanse us from all wickedness.

—1 John 1:9

A mom had been trying to teach her young son how to use a nondigital clock—you know, the kind with the big hand and the little hand. For several days she kept talking to him about the "big hand" and the "little hand." One day she heard the little boy walk into the kitchen, where there was a clock on the wall.

"Cameron!" she called out from the other room. "What is the little hand on?"

"A chocolate chip cookie!" he yelled back.

Oops! That little boy was caught with his little hand in the cookie jar—literally!

Sometimes we find ourselves caught with our hand in the cookie jar. Maybe we're caught telling a lie. Or cheating. Or saying unkind words to our sister. We feel bad about being caught—and we also feel bad about *what* we've been caught doing or saying. Getting caught is no fun at all!

The best thing to do when we get caught with our hand in the cookie jar is to go to Jesus. While He might disapprove of what we've done, He'll never disapprove of who we are. Jesus condemns our sin, but He never condemns *us*.

Jesus loves us just the way we are, but He loves us too much to let us stay with our hand caught in the cookie jar. Once we confess our sin to Him and tell Him we're sorry, He gives us His grace and removes our guilt. And that leads to goodness—us telling someone else we're sorry and making that relationship stronger and better than ever.

▶ **Jesus, thank You that I can always turn to You when I do something wrong. I know that if I confess my sin, You will always forgive me.**

Take This with You

Jesus will always forgive us, always love us, and always accept us.

Helping the Hurting

So let us come boldly to the throne of our gracious
God. There we will receive his mercy, and we will
find grace to help us when we need it most.

—Hebrews 4:16

Have you ever been so close to a famous person that you could almost reach out and touch them? That happened to me when I went to a golf tournament and found myself standing super close to the great golfer Tiger Woods. I actually reached out my hand to pat him on the shoulder—until he looked me right in the eyes, as if to say, "Don't you even think about it!"

Later on, I thought about how I didn't even think of getting Tiger Woods's autograph. I just wanted to touch him because he was so amazing!

You're not a famous golfer, but I'm sure some people look up to you. Think about the kid at school who eats lunch alone or the girl on your soccer team who doesn't really talk to anyone. Lots of kids feel alone and like they don't matter. They need someone to be kind to them and to include them, and they might be wondering if that someone is you.

Jesus would have reached out to them, so He expects us to do the same.

When Jesus was living here on earth, people who were hurting or suffering were drawn to Him and just wanted to touch Him and be noticed by Him. They wanted two things from Jesus—help and hope. Whenever someone touched Jesus, He stopped. He responded to them. He didn't ignore anyone. He let hurting people know, "You're important, even if nobody else thinks you are."

We're called to be like Jesus and to share His grace and love with others.

▶ **Jesus, show me those around me who need help and hope.**

Take This with You

If I know Jesus, I should treat hurting people the way Jesus would treat them.

44

Include Everyone

For I have come to call not those who think they are
righteous, but those who know they are sinners.

—Matthew 9:13

If you try to imagine what kind of people would have been best friends with Jesus, you might imagine people who were perfect—or at least pretty close to perfect. After all, why would someone like Jesus want to hang out with losers?

The reality is that the people who hung out with Jesus were totally *not* perfect. People who felt unloved by everybody else felt loved by Jesus. He was willing to hang out with them and talk to them and listen to their problems—even if nobody else would.

The more those who are not followers of Christ are loved by those of us who are followers of Christ, the more open they may be to following Christ. We need to show them a picture of Christ by loving them, respecting them, and treating them with kindness.

I'm not saying you should look for the kids who are mean to others or the kids who are disrespectful to adults and only choose those kids as your friends. You need to hang out with people who are a good influence on you and who make the right choices. But you also need to realize that nobody is perfect—not you, not anyone!

Jesus wants you to include the people who are rejected. He wants you to talk to that girl who's always standing by herself at swim practice. He wants you to be friendly to the boy who doesn't speak English very well. He wants you to include your younger sibling in the game, even if others are telling little kids they can't play.

When you have Jesus in your life, He leads you to include everyone.

▶ **Jesus, help me to notice and include those who are rejected by others.**

Take This with You

Even though Jesus was perfect, He didn't hang out with perfect people. He included everyone.

45

Being Great

Whoever wants to be a leader among
you must be your servant.

—Matthew 20:26

What is the greatest book of all time? The greatest movie? The greatest song? Who was the greatest basketball player? The greatest president? The greatest actor?

If you ask a group of people one of these questions, you're definitely going to get a lively discussion going—and maybe a big argument! Why? Because there's no real definition of "the greatest"—you'll get all different opinions.

When we think of greatness, we think of what someone has accomplished or how successful they are. The people we tend to call *great* are people who either *have* a lot or have *done* a lot. But God has a different definition of greatness. There's a difference between doing great things and being a great person.

Jesus says true greatness isn't about success. It's about *service*.

The world measures greatness by how many people serve you. Jesus measures greatness by how many people you serve. The world measures greatness by who is in first place.

Jesus measures greatness by who is in last place. The world measures greatness by how much we get. Jesus measures greatness by how much we give.

In a world where everybody wants to be first, it's hard to imagine greatness as being last. But that's what Jesus said in Mark 9:35: "Whoever wants to be first must take last place and be the servant of everyone else."

To Jesus, greatness doesn't come from how many blue ribbons or first-place trophies you get. It comes from how much and how many you serve. And it doesn't matter how many people notice you serving. It doesn't matter if *anyone* notices you serving. You can help a mom play with her fidgety toddler. You can clear the dinner table without being asked. You can help your teacher staple papers or clean off the whiteboard.

By serving others, you become great in God's eyes.

▶ **Jesus, help me to think of others and to serve them.**

Take This with You

The moment you choose to serve others,
God says, "You are great."

46

A Servant First

I have given you an example to follow.
Do as I have done to you.

—John 13:15

What would you do if someone came up to you with the nastiest, dirtiest, stinkiest feet you'd ever seen? You'd probably say, "Yuck! Get those feet away from me!" You probably *wouldn't* say, "Hey, let me wash your feet and then dry them off with my favorite towel."

Most of us can't think of many things more disgusting than touching someone else's filthy feet. But that's what Jesus did for His friends! At that time, what Jesus did was only done by slaves. And Jesus was the Son of God.

When Jesus washed His disciples' feet, He was teaching them a few things. First, He was teaching them that *nobody* is too great to serve. Who could be greater than the Son of God? Nobody! And yet He was willing to kneel down and serve others. He was also teaching them that He is the one who makes us clean. When we surrender our dirty lives to Him, He bathes us in His grace and love and forgiveness.

God wants us to live a life of service to Him. And serving Him means serving others. It means washing feet.

Okay, okay, you don't have to go around with soap and a towel and demand that people take off their shoes and socks so you can wash their feet. (That would be kind of weird, anyway!) But you *can* look for ways to help others, even if it means getting your own hands a little bit dirty in the process. If Jesus served others, we can too!

▶ **Jesus, help me to do things for others, even things I don't really want to do.**

Take This with You

Jesus says it is better to serve than to be served.

47

Winning Against Temptation

Resist the devil, and he will flee from you.

—James 4:7

Have you ever been tempted to tell a lie or talk back to your parents or spread some gossip? We've all been tempted to do something wrong. Being tempted isn't the big thing—it's whether we give in to that temptation. If we give in, we've lost. But if we resist the temptation, we win. And God has promised to help us win.

A lot of people confuse temptation with sin, but it's not a sin to be tempted. When someone is being tempted, it doesn't mean they don't have Jesus in their life. After all, Jesus Himself was tempted when He was living on earth. He was the Son of God and He did exactly what His Father wanted him to do. But He still had to face temptation.

Jesus spent forty days in the wilderness being tempted by the devil. Talk about rough! And He was tempted in three different ways. First, He was tempted *physically*. He had been fasting—not eating—for forty days, and I bet He was ready for a double cheeseburger and a milkshake! But Jesus didn't give in.

Second, Jesus was tempted *emotionally*. The devil tried

to mess with His thoughts and feelings. But He didn't give in.

Finally, Jesus was tempted *spiritually*. Satan tried to mess with His relationship with God. Again, Jesus refused to give in. And He won!

So what was Jesus's secret? How was He able to say no to Satan every time when Satan kept bugging and bugging Him? Jesus had two secret weapons to fight temptation. And they're the same ones we have today. Jesus was led by the Holy Spirit, and He was also armed with the Scriptures. We can turn to the same two sources when we're tempted. If we pray and read the Word of God, we'll be able to win against temptation every time.

▶ **Jesus, thank You for giving me Your Spirit and Your Word so I can say no every time I'm tempted to do wrong.**

Take This with You

Jesus helps me overcome temptation.

48

All In

If any of you wants to be my follower, you must turn from your selfish ways, take up your cross daily, and follow me.

—Luke 9:23

Have you ever jumped off a super high diving board? It's not something you can do halfway. You can't step over the edge of the board and then decide, *Oops! I don't want to do this. I'm going back.* Nope! Once you've made that commitment to jump, it's happening. You can't go back. You're all in!

Jesus is all about being all in for God. He says there's no other way to live your life. Becoming one of His followers means you're ready to follow Him. There's no going back. You're not going to do things *your* way anymore. You're going to do things *His* way. You're all in!

Life is not all about *you* anymore. It's about loving God and loving others and following what God's Word says you should do.

You've probably studied early explorers in school. One of them, Hernando Cortes of Spain, came to Mexico in 1519. He had been given orders to conquer the land and build a colony. When all his men had gotten off the boats, he did something that seemed kind of crazy—and maybe a little risky. He burned the boats. There was no going back. He and his crew were all in.

That's the only way to follow Jesus—all in!

▷ **Jesus, I'm convinced You are worth going all in. Help me to trust You and follow You every day of my life.**

Take This with You

When I go all in for Jesus, I can experience the awesome new life He has for me.

49

Clues That Are True

When we were utterly helpless, Christ came at
just the right time and died for us sinners.

—Romans 5:6.

Have you ever played the game of Clue? As you go through the game and eliminate clues that aren't true, you narrow things down to what *is* true. The first one to figure out which Clue cards are in the secret envelope wins the game.

The Bible has given us a whole bunch of clues that what Jesus said was true. Way back in the Old Testament, a ton of prophecies foretold Jesus's coming.

Isaiah 7:14 announces that the virgin Mary would give birth to a son who would be called Immanuel.

Micah 5:2 says the Messiah would come from Bethlehem, and Luke 2:1-7 tells us Jesus *was* born in Bethlehem.

Psalm 22:6 predicts that the Messiah's hands and feet would be pierced, which they were at His crucifixion.

These are just a few of over three hundred prophecies—or clues that were true—that Jesus fulfilled. They prove that Jesus is the Son of God.

The more you read your Bible, the more you'll be

convinced that Jesus is who He says He is—the Son of God who saves us from our sins. And when you believe He is telling the truth about who He says He is, you win the game!

▶ **Jesus, thank You for dying on the cross for my sins. Help me to know that everything You say is truth.**

Take This with You

The Bible gives me enough clues that Jesus is the Son of God for me to know it is the truth.

50

He Died for Me

For this is how God loved the world: He gave his
one and only Son, so that everyone who believes
in him will not perish but have eternal life.

—John 3:16

What's the biggest thing someone has ever done for you?

Maybe your dad works overtime to afford piano lessons for you. Perhaps your mom homeschools you and your siblings. Or your whole family eats differently because you're allergic to some foods.

When someone does something for you, it often means they give up something else. Your dad gave up some free time so you could have those piano lessons. Your mom gave up a job she really liked so she could teach you. Your family gave up cinnamon rolls or ice cream so you would have an easier time avoiding the foods that are bad for you.

Jesus did the most amazing thing for us ever—and He definitely gave something up—when He died on the cross for our sins. This is something He knew He was going to do a long, long time before it happened. Before you and I were even born, and before this world was even created, God knew Jesus would take our punishment so we could have eternal life.

Death on the cross wasn't a surprise to Jesus. He knew it was coming, and He could have stopped it if He'd wanted to. But He wanted to give up the most precious thing of all—His life—to give us the most precious thing of all—eternal life.

Aren't you happy He made that choice?

▶ **Jesus, thank You for giving up Your life to give me eternal life.**

Take This with You

Jesus gave me the most amazing thing ever when He died on the cross for my sins.

51

An Unexpected Hero

He personally carried our sins in his body on the
cross so that we can be dead to sin and live for
what is right. By his wounds you are healed.

—1 Peter 2:24

When you hear the word *warrior*, what do you think of?
A superhero? A knight in shining armor? Your favorite sci-fi hero?

Way back at the beginning of time, God promised His people He would send them a warrior who would defeat the enemy, Satan. It was just one prophecy, but the people began to picture a mighty warrior who would come in and take over.

When He did come, a lot of people didn't think Jesus seemed like a mighty warrior. After all, He hung out with the poor and He Himself didn't seem very wealthy or powerful. He wasn't what many of the people expected, but those who did choose to follow Him understood He was the Son of God and their long-awaited Messiah.

Now imagine the shock and total confusion when everyone who believed Jesus was their king saw Him being handed over to be crucified. Suddenly many of them started to wonder, "Could Jesus really be God's warrior?"

Jesus, though, knew there was only one weapon that could defeat the enemy. The only way to fight sin and death was for God to sacrifice His Son.

There's only one way to get to heaven. You can't get there by being a good person. You can't get there by going to church every single Sunday. You can't get there by paying your way. The only way to get there is to ask Jesus to come into your heart and to forgive you for your sins and to help you live every day the way He wants you to live. After all, He's a true hero—the truest hero that ever lived—and it's the best thing in the world to have Him on your side.

▶ **Jesus, thank You for being the true hero who died for our sins and rose again to free us from sin and death.**

Take This with You

The best thing in the world
is to have Jesus on my side.

52

There's Hope!

I am the resurrection and the life. Anyone who believes in me will live, even after dying.

—John 11:25

Have you ever been frustrated trying to do something you've never done before? It's super tempting to just give up. You wonder if it's even worth it and if there's any hope!

Don't worry—there's always hope! Because Jesus faced and overcame death, He gives hope to all of us. And we're not just talking about the hope that there is life after death (as important as that is!), but also that Jesus gives us hope for this life we're living right now.

Jesus gives us hope that the things we do today do matter. Your life does make a difference here on earth. Your words of kindness make a difference. Your cheerful, helpful attitude makes a difference. Your hard work makes a difference.

We also need hope that there is more to life than the things we're doing today, as important as they may be. If we look at the big picture, everything we do today is pointing us toward tomorrow—and eventually our life with Jesus in heaven. That's why He wants us to follow Him during this life.

God tells us through the truth of His Word that there's always hope if we put our trust in Jesus. All that we hope for, all that we need, can be found in Him.

▶ **Jesus, thank You that You will always give me hope.**

Take This with You

The best place for me to put my hope is in Jesus.